MW01488666

THE

KINGDOM

OF

GOD

SERMON BASED SMALL GROUP GUIDE

WRITTEN BY

JOHN CAMPBELL

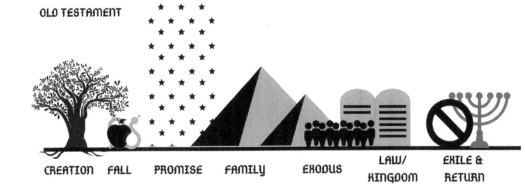

OLD TESTAMENT

CREATION   FALL   PROMISE   FAMILY   EXODUS   LAW/   EXILE &
                                                   KINGDOM   RETURN

CONTENTS

March 3   The Road of the Kingdom   7

March 10   The Door of the Kingdom   13

March 17   The Way of the Kingdom   19

March 24   The Grace of the Kingdom   25

March 31   The Work of the Kingdom   31

April 7   The People of the Kingdom   35

April 14   The Hope of the Kingdom   41

April 21   The Arrival of the Kingdom   47

April 28   The Mission of the Kingdom   49

May 5   The Kingdom for Every Nation   53

May 12   The Kingdom for All Peoples   59

May 19   The Kingdom for Every Person   63

May 26   The Kingdom for Sinners   69

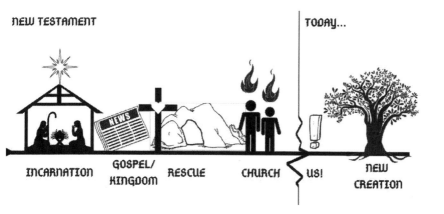

NEW TESTAMENT   TODAY...

INCARNATION   GOSPEL/ KINGDOM   RESCUE   CHURCH   US!   NEW CREATION

But seek first the Kingdom of God and his righteousness,
and all these things will be added to you.

Matthew 6:33

the road of the kingdom

—

"All I know is I'm not home yet. This is not where I belong. Take this world and give me Jesus, this is not where I belong."

These lyrics from a song called, "Where I Belong," by the Christian band Building 429 express a sentiment held by many Christians in our world today. They point to the awareness that we all have that the world is broken, painful, and not what God intended when he created everything and called it, "good." They also point to the deep desire that we have to experience that garden, that goodness, and be with Christ in heaven – free from our pain, free from our suffering, and free from everything in this life that is difficult.

Here's the problem…

In our scripture today, Jesus speaks to his disciples and makes one thing very clear. The cross to which he was heading wouldn't just define his future, it would define theirs as well.[1]

---

[1] Turner, D.L. (2008) Baker Exegetical Commentary on the New Testament: Matthew. Grand Rapids, MI: Baker Academic.

Our text today pushes firmly against the idea that Christians are not meant for this world or that we do not belong here. It pushes against the idea of escapism and our selfish desires to leave behind the pains of this world so that we can feel better while others are left to suffer and die. Most importantly, the text reveals to us why the suffering is worth it, why the pain is worth it, and why the world is in desperate need for Christians to be present in the world instead of trying to escape it.

Read Matthew 16:24-25. After predicting his own death, Jesus speaks these words to his disciples, explaining exactly what following him, being his disciple, or having salvation will look like.

How would you say what Jesus just said in your own words? What do you hear him saying?

Is this generally in line with how the world influences us to think and act? How or how not?

Is this generally in line with how the Church influences us to think and act? How or how not?

Jesus is saying, "Self-preservation in the present life will lead to ultimate destruction. Self-denial will lead to ultimate self-fulfillment. If you think you can avoid the cross, you will lose your life, but if you embrace the cross, you will find your life."

How does self-preservation lead to our destruction? Can you think of specific ways that we do this?

What do you think self-denial that leads to self-fulfillment looks like? What examples can you think of?

Read Matthew 16:26. In your own words, what do you hear Jesus saying?

What are the ways that we try to gain the whole world? Name specific examples.

If Jesus is correct, and these things neither bring us acceptance from God or help us to experience what it means to be truly human, why do we pursue them with so much effort? Why do we desire them?

Read Matthew 16:27-28. What do you hear Jesus saying to his disciples here?

Jesus is trying to help his disciples be prepared for his coming death on the cross, not just for their personal comfort, but so that they would be prepared to carry on his kingdom mission in his absence.

He doesn't want them to be so flustered and crushed by the difficulties and hardships ahead of them that they stop doing everything that he trained them to do.

In other words, Jesus is saying – no matter how bad it gets, remember: you belong here. I want you here. You are the people who I am entrusting my mission to. You are the people that are going to show the world what everything is going to be like when I return.

How does escapism prevent us from living out the mission Christ has given us?

Read Matthew 17:1-8. *The story of the transfiguration is this incredible moment where Jesus' disciples get a glimpse of the glory that Christ just spoke of. They get to see a picture of what is coming.* The moment is so amazing, so powerful, how does Peter react? Why do you think he reacts this way?

What happens as Peter speaks? What does God say?

Do you think that it is any coincidence that this command from God for us to listen to Jesus comes just six days after Jesus telling his disciples that the only way to follow him was to follow the same path of suffering and hardship that he endured? Why or why not?

The road to heaven will always go through the cross of Jesus Christ. If we want to have him, have life, and have heaven, we have to lower ourselves like he lowered himself. We have to serve like he served. We have to enter pain and suffering instead of avoiding it. We have to give instead of take. We have to seek the fulfillment of others instead of the fulfillment of ourselves. We have to die so that we might live.

This was the message of Jesus. And God says, "Listen to him."

Based on these instructions given to us by Jesus, how would you describe life in the Kingdom of God?

What is one practical thing that you will do this week to help yourself and others experience that kingdom now?

the door of the kingdom

—

"I think it's a moral obligation to mind your own business."

"Counting other people's sins does not make you a saint."

"Let people do what they need to do to be happy. Mind your own business and do what you need to do to make you happy."

"My life. My choices. My mistakes. My lessons. Not your business."

Do you agree with the sentiment of these statements? Why or why not?

A quick Google search brought up these and many more quotes that express a central belief within our western, individualistic culture... If everyone would just mind their own business, everyone would be happy, and everything would be better.

Read Matthew 18:15. These are Jesus' words to his followers. Where do you think Jesus stands on the whole "mind your own business" idea?

Who does Jesus instruct us to correct? Why is this important?

Do you expect your fellow Christians to point your sin out to you? Why or why not?

Read Matthew 18:15-17. What is the process Jesus lays out for how we should address the sin in each other's lives?

What elements of the process seem important or stand out to you?

How is this different from how we typically deal with each other's sins?

How might this process lead to healthy repentance?

As we deal with each other's sinfulness, what should always be our ultimate goal?

How does the process given by Jesus help work towards this?

Read verse 17 again. How do you feel about Jesus' statement here?

Who specifically is Jesus telling us not to associate with?

(non-repentant Christians)

Why do you think Jesus goes there? Why would associating with these people be so bad?

Do you believe that the Church should distance itself from unrepentant Christians? Why or why not?

Why is this so hard to do in our world and culture today?

Read Matthew 7:3-5. What do you hear Jesus saying?

How would our own willingness to be held accountable to our sins create an environment of forgiveness, reconciliation, and grace that might lend to the process Jesus is talking about?

What does Jesus' teaching on sin teach us about what the Kingdom of God will be like?

What is the plank in your own eye today? What sins do you tear others down for that you commit yourself?

What is one specific thing that your group (the church) could do to help you repent and experience the kingdom even today?

the way of the kingdom

Matthew 20:1-16

—

Just a few years ago, I received the invitation from another man to "step outside" behind a restaurant in West Virginia for a good old-fashioned fight. I declined, but our text today reminds me of that moment in my life.

The invitation was proceeded by the man cutting a long line of restaurant patrons waiting to pay their bill. As I watched the man cut, I could also see several other people in line grow uncomfortable and disgruntled, but no one spoke up. So, I did.

"The line starts back there," I informed the man, which quickly led to his desire to fight me.

I remember the whole situation very well, but most vivid are the memories of how I felt before I spoke up. I felt justified in calling the man out. We had been standing in that line long before he entered the room. It wasn't right – it wasn't fair for him to just walk in and cut. Unfortunately, for me, it is that same sense of entitlement and "justice" that Jesus addresses in our story this morning.

Read Matthew 20:1-12. How would you summarize what has happened so far in the story?

How would you feel if you were one of the workers hired first thing in the morning?

Read Matthew 20:13-16. In your own words, how does the landowner respond?

As he started to tell this story, Jesus tells us that the story is a description of the kingdom of heaven. Let's look at that:

Who do you think the landowner represents?

Who do you think the workers hired before the afternoon represent?

Who do you think the last workers hired represent?

Based on all of this, what do you think the point of Jesus' story is? What does it teach us about the kingdom of heaven?

Jesus' death and resurrection would bring grace and forgiveness, not just to the Jews, but to all people. Jews, Gentiles, people of all races and ethnicities. For the Jews, this was a hard message to see, let alone learn and believe.

Let's start big: How do we do the same thing? Are there still "gentiles" that we exclude from the Good News of Jesus Christ today? Who and how so?

Let's get closer to home: How do we do this in our own church?

Are there any members of your group that are relatively new to our church compared to others? Ask them: Are they treated as equals to long-term members? Do we listen to or involve them as much? Give them grace and space to answer honestly.

Are there long-term members of our church in your group? Ask them: Do they feel like we pay more attention to guests and new members more than them? How does that make them feel? Give them grace and space to answer as well.

Should we treat each other differently based on how old or young, new or tenured we are in the faith? Why or why not?

Read Matthew 20:20-28. Almost immediately after Jesus tells the parable of the workers, Jesus' own disciples get in a dispute of which of them deserves to sit at his right and at his left. Who matters the most? Who gets the biggest reward? How does Jesus respond?

What might be different in our church if we each did a better job of trying to serve one another instead of being served?

How might our community benefit from us trying to serve them where and how they are instead of trying to attract them to us to become like us?

How would all of this better reveal what the kingdom of God is like to the world?

What is one thing that you will do this week to serve someone that you typically expect to be served by?

the grace of the kingdom

Matthew 22:1-14

Have you ever planned a party? It can create a lot of work. Where will you gather? What will you eat? Where will everyone sit? How will you keep everyone entertained?

Have you ever planned a party that no one showed up to? Imagine how you would feel. The time, work and money that you had lost would matter, but would it be as bad as the feeling of rejection?

Jesus' parable of the wedding banquet draws upon these types of emotions to point to something very, very big within his ministry. The Israelites were God's chosen people, but they were rejecting God's own Son. They were the bridegroom, rejecting the groom God had chosen for them.

As a result, God was opening up the gates. His covenant and promise, his salvation, was going to go out into all the world!

But beware. This wonderful story of inclusion ends with a shocking twist… one that we all should pay very close attention to.

Has anyone ever planned an event of a party that no one came to? How did that make you feel?

Read Matthew 22:1-14. Who are the characters of the story and who do they represent?

The King:_____ The Son: _____

The Servants: _____ The invited: _____

Those on the street corners: _____

The guests at the party: _____

With our characters defined, what do you think the overall message of this parable is?

How does the king display both extreme generosity and very harsh judgement?

Are you comfortable with Jesus describing God like this? Why or why not?

Read Matthew 22:2-6 again. Why did people refuse to come to the banquet? What were they focused on instead?

How do you make this same mistake today?

What priorities in your life need reordered or replaced?

Read Matthew 22:11-14 again. This man actually came to the banquet! Why is the king so upset? (Hint – this has nothing to do with how you dress when you come to church.)

Read Titus 2:11-14. Paul tells us that the grace of God has appeared and offered salvation to ALL people. What does Paul say grace teaches us to do?

How does this connect to how the king reacts in Jesus' parable?

Why do you think people reject Christ's invitation into grace?

Jesus' parable teaches us that the invitation into the Kingdom of God has been given to everyone – all peoples. But, not everyone, even people who go to church every week, will have salvation. The evidence of our salvation – the wedding clothes that we wear to the banquet – are godliness, self-control, holiness, and an eagerness to do what is good.

As you look at your own life, are there ways that you are rejecting God's grace? In other words, where are you saying "yes" to ungodliness and worldly passions?

What does Jesus' teachings about grace and holiness tell us about what life in the Kingdom of God is be like?

What is one thing that you could do this week to begin saying, "No," to worldly passions and to begin saying, "yes," to life in the kingdom?

the work of the kingdom

—

John Wooden, one of the most accomplished college basketball coaches in history is credited with saying, "Confidence comes from being prepared."

Coach Wooden was talking about basketball, but his words transcend into life and faith and press upon a question that all Christians ask at some point: How do I know that I am saved?

Jesus' Parable of the Ten Virgins is not a call to be watchful. It is a call to be prepared. The two are different, as we will discuss in our lesson today.

Read Matthew 25:1-13. In this parable, the bridegroom represents Jesus and the ten virgins are us, his followers. Knowing that, what do you think the overall message of Jesus' parable is?

In verse 5, Jesus tells us that all 10 virgins fell asleep while they waited, but he doesn't chastise this. The fools were those without oil when the bridegroom arrived. What is the difference between watchfulness and preparedness?

Which do you think Jesus is advocating for in this story?

It is interesting that all ten of the virgins believed that the bridegroom was coming. They all went out to meet him. Isn't belief enough? What do you think?

What do you think Jesus is teaching us about the relationship between belief and works?

Read James 2:14-19. What does James say about faith and works?

What are some examples of how we watch for Jesus, but remain unprepared for his coming?

What are the empty torches that we carry around today that might be deceiving us into thinking we are prepared?

What is the oil that would indicate true preparedness? What kind of works evidence true belief?

If you could only be judged based on your actions, not your beliefs, would you be considered wise or foolish in our parable today? Why?

What does Jesus' teaching on faith and action teach us about what life is like in the Kingdom of God?

What is one practical thing that you will do this week *because you believe in Jesus that* will help you be prepared for the arrival of his kingdom?

the people of the kingdom

Matthew 25:31-46

—

When I was a student at Purdue University, two of my brothers visited me and we attended a concert together. My little brother, now an Indiana University alumnus, was wearing a read IU baseball hat. As we were leaving the concert, a random Purdue student walked past us and slapped the bill of my little brother's hat, said something inappropriate and profane, and knocked the hat backwards off of his head.

In that moment, an instinct rose up within me and I felt a surge of anger and adrenaline.

I've always loved my brother. We have always (mostly) gotten along. But I had never felt like this. I became protective. My little brother had been mistreated and it was as if that student had knocked the hat off of my head, not his. This wasn't just an offense against him, it was an offense against me.

Nothing came of my anger. There was no revenge. My little brother, in his laid-back nature, seemed less upset than I was and calmed the situation quickly. I was so upset that it had happened, but today, I am incredibly thankful for that moment in my life.

I am thankful because of how it helps me understand our text today. Jesus, in the midst of challenging the religious leaders of Israel and denouncing Israel because of their false religion and disobedience, makes an incredible claim. It is a claim that there is a new Israel, not made up of the religious elite, but of those who do the will of his Father. Those people, Jesus says, are his brothers and sisters, and woe to anyone who mistreats them...

Read Matthew 25:31-46. How would you summarize this parable? What do you think is the big statement Jesus is trying to make?

Read verse 40 again. In the Jewish faith, anyone born of Abraham – any Jew – would be considered your brother or sister. In Matthew 12:50, Jesus says, "Whoever does the will of my Father in heaven is my brother and sister and mother." Why would this be offensive to many Jews?

We often think of the sheep and the goats as representing believers and non-believers, but Jesus is speaking to and talking about people who all would have said that they believed in God.

In the shepherd culture that Jesus was speaking to, separating the sheep from the goats was a nightly task that many of his listeners would be very familiar with. It was also a task that wasn't always easy. The sheep and the goats were hard to tell apart. Sometimes, the only visual difference was a tail that pointed up (goat) vs. a tail that pointed down (sheep.)

The only difference between the sheep and the goats in Jesus' story is what they did and did not do in their lives. What is the telltale sign that Jesus will use to tell the sheep from the goats?

Why do you think Jesus makes caring for the hungry, the thirsty, the stranger, the naked, the sick, and the imprisoned – the weak, vulnerable, and needy – the primary issue by which he will judge his followers?

In Jesus' parable, the goats were the religious Jews who went to the temple, wore the right clothes, made the right sacrifices, sang the right songs, prayed the right prayers, and knew all of the scriptures. They were visible and lauded in their communities as being devote Jews, but they didn't love and care for other people.

The sheep were also very likely to be regular participants in the activities of the Jewish religion, but they were not as visible or celebrated because they were less concerned about others seeing them and were more concerned about serving others.

As you think about these two categories, who are usually more visible and listened to in the church today? Why do you think so?

Is this healthy or bad? Why do you think so?

Read verse 46 again. What is the outcome for those judged to be goats?

Jesus has a deep, passionate love for those that he calls his brothers and sisters and he has a fierce, righteous anger that burns within him when his siblings are mistreated. How do we ignore and mistreat each other – even by using our religion to do so - within the church?

If judgement came today, would you be confident that how you are treating others would result in Jesus calling you his brother or sister? Why or why not?

What does Jesus' teaching about the sheep and the goats teach us about what life is like in the Kingdom of God?

What is one practical thing that you could do this week to help reveal His kingdom by serving someone else and caring for those in need?

What is something that you could to together as a group?

the hope of the kingdom

Matthew 21:1-11;

—

I had a friend in high school who was a super fan of the Indianapolis Colts. He adored them. On the spot, during any season, he could rattle off the entire team roster, including the practice squad, without hesitation. When he turned eighteen, his first act as an adult was to get the Colts logo tattooed on his arm.

One of his most prized possessions was a Colts football helmet that was covered in autographs. He had personally obtained signatures from every single player on the team – except one. No matter how hard he tried, he could not get this elusive signature.

One day, while the Colts were holding training camp here in Terre Haute, my friend just so happened to be walking across the campus where the practices were being held, carrying his helmet, with a marker in his pocket, and rounded a corner and ran right into that player.

It was perfect. It was meant to be – maybe even divine.

As he introduced himself, holding out the helmet and marker, he began to ask for the player's autograph. Before he could even finish, the player said, "No, man," and walked away.

There's an old saying, "Don't ever meet your hero's."

The idea is that you will always be disappointed. The person might be shorter than you imagined, not quite as handsome, and maybe even a jerk. From a distance, we idolize other people and when we finally come face to face, eventually, reality hits us hard.

The story of the triumphal entry is such a story.

Read Matthew 21:1-11. How does the gathering crowd respond to Jesus' arrival? How do they treat him?

In 2 Kings 9, Jehu is anointed king of Israel even though there was already a king in place. The people, longing for a release from the corruption and violence of the standing king, quickly took off their cloaks and spread them out for Jehu to walk on. This was surely on the minds of those laying out their cloaks for Jesus. What do you think the crowds were hoping for politically by choosing Jesus as king?

The crowds also laid out and waved branches that they cut off of the trees around them. About 200 years before the triumphal entry, the Jews did the same thing to welcome Judas Maccabaeus into Israel after he led an army that conquered invading enemies and freed Israel from their oppression. What do you think the crowds were hoping for nationally by choosing Jesus as king?

The crowds also shouted, "Hosanna," which is a phrase drawn from the Psalms that means, "O Save," as they called Jesus, "the Son of David." David symbolized the golden age of Israel as a people and as a nation. What do you think the crowds were hoping for economically by choosing Jesus as king?

Jesus was welcomed into Jerusalem by a massive throng of people who celebrated him as a king – a king who would conquer Israel's enemies and bring prosperity, comfort, and safety to Israel.

Read Matthew 27:32-46.

Days later, Jesus is hung on a cross, his kingship mocked as a crown of thorns is nailed into his head, as insults are spit out at him, as his followers have all abandoned him, and Jesus is left to cry out to God, "Why have you forsaken me." Jesus was utterly and devastatingly alone.

Why do you think the crowds were so quick to run to Jesus and then so quick to leave him to die?

What do think Jesus' real mission was as he rode into Jerusalem?

How did hopes of the Israelites differ from the work that Jesus actually came to do?

Have ever been disappointed by God because he didn't meet your expectations? What happened?

What are some expectations that we place on God that are unrealistic? What do we hope for that God never promised?

As Jesus entered Jerusalem, his destination as the cross. What does this teach us about what we are supposed to hope for in the kingdom of God?

This week, take time to evaluate your relationship with God and answer the following questions on your own.

Why did you seek salvation? Was it to simply know God or to get things from God?

How often do you pray? What does that say about how much you desire a relationship with God?

What do you pray for? Do you ask for what you want or for what God wants? Do you ever just try to listen? Or is your prayer always one sided? What does your prayer life teach you about how much you desire a relationship with God?

How well do you obey (or even try to obey) Jesus' commands? What does your obedience teach you about how much you desire a relationship with God?

As you look at your answers, what is it that you are hoping for?

Prosperity, comfort, and safety?

Or the rescue from sin and death so that you can know and be known by God?

the arrival of the kingdom

Matthew 28:1-10

—

Christ is risen!

No other phrase has shaped the hope, joy, and mission of the people of God like this one. Christ is risen! With every uttering, with every announcement of this amazing truth, we proclaim the Good News of Jesus Christ to the world. We proclaim freedom to those in bondage, justice to the oppressed, power to the powerless, and life to the dead.

Easter is not just a story about what happened in Jerusalem 2,000 years ago. Easter is a promise of what is happening right now, all around us, and of what is still yet to come.

Easter is about resurrection. Jesus didn't renew Israel. He created a new Israel. Jesus doesn't fix us or change us. Jesus brings us to life for the very first time. And when he returns, when we see that glory, we will experience the fullness of the resurrection that he has already began in us.

This week, our lesson will be quite different. You'll notice there's not a lot of material. That's because we want you to provide the material…

Before you panic – we're not asking for a deep, Biblical study based on hours of theological study… we're just asking for your resurrection story.

This week, all we really want you to do is to celebrate Easter - celebrate the resurrection of Jesus – by celebrating each other's resurrections. Whether your salvation story is short and simple, long and complicated, recent or from a time long, long ago… take the time today to go through your group and have each person share how they came to know Christ.

As you do, take time to pray for each person, thanking God for his presence in their lives, for the ways that he worked to reveal himself to them, and for the new life that he has given them in Jesus Christ.

the mission of the kingdom

Matthew 28:16-20

—

Every Sunday is Easter Sunday.

The early church believed this and worshipped like this. The reality and result of the resurrection of Jesus Christ shaped everything that they did. His resurrection not only guaranteed their eternal future, it determined what they gave their lives to every single day.

And what was that purpose? What was that mission that was shaped by the truth of Easter? We discover it in some of Jesus' last words to his followers before his ascent into heaven. We call it these words the Great Commission and they are the Christ commanded mission of every single one of his followers until the moment he returns.

Read Matthew 28:16-20. Based on this text, how would you describe God's heart for the world? What does he want for his creation?

Read Acts 1:8. To where does God send us to fulfill the Great Commission?

Think about where you are. The people you know. The world you live in. In each of these areas, who is God calling you to reach?

Jerusalem: (your church, your family, your closest friends)

Judea: (your work, your acquaintances, your neighbors, etc.)

Samaria: (people you know, but who are religiously, culturally, racially, or ethnically different than you)

Ends of the earth: (the whole world, all people groups)

If you couldn't think of someone for each category, why do you think that is?

Most Christians do not witness to, disciple, or teach everything that Christ commanded to even their closest family and friends, let alone to the ends of the earth. Why do you think that is?

Read Romans 10:1, 12-15. *Paul's heart's desire and prayer to God was that people might be saved. He longed deeply for this to be true. It grieved him that there were people – even his enemies - who didn't know Jesus like he did.*

Could you honestly say that your heart's desire and prayer to God is that others may be saved? Before you answer… how often do you pray for the salvation of others, in general or for specific individuals?

If we could only answer this question based on your actions, on how much you were out sharing the Good News with others, making disciples, and teaching others to obey Jesus… what would our conclusion be?

What does Jesus' final command to his followers teach us about what life is like in the kingdom of God?

What is one practical thing that you will do this week to fulfill the Great Commission?

Who is one person that you will commit to praying for so that they might know God?

the kingdom for every nation

Acts 10:1-17; 34-48

—

In one of his commentaries on the book of Acts, N.T. Wright encourages us to, "Imagine a mother seeing her child at the other side of the street, about to cross a busy road. 'Stand still,' she shouts urgently. Then, a minute later, seeing that the traffic has come to a stop at the light, she shouts again, 'Walk across!'

She hasn't contradicted herself," Wright points out, saying, "The initial command was the right one for the time… It is because she wanted the child to walk across in the end that she told him to stand still for the moment. If he hadn't, he wouldn't have made it across at all."[2]

Wright uses that story to point to what is happening in our text this morning. As Jesus' first followers started going out into the world to participate in the Great Commission, they had to learn a very important lesson. The Good News that Jesus sent them out to share was not limited to any one nation. God was calling children to himself out of Israel and, now, even out of Israel's greatest enemy at the time: Rome.

---

[2] Wright, N.T. (2008). Acts for Everyone. Westminster John Knox Press. Louisville, KY.

This is shocking news. Not only because Rome was considered to be evil and pagan and immoral, but because God had chosen Israel out of all the nations. They were his treasured possession.

The very laws and rules that segregated and separated Israel from non-Jews like the Romans were created and commanded by God himself.

But, if God was going to get what he had always intended for the world, Peter and the rest of Jesus' followers would have to learn that the Gospel wasn't just for the Israelites, it was for every nation. What God had commanded for a particular period and for a particular purpose was no longer useful. The initial command was the right one for the time... but a new command had been given.

Read Acts 10:1-8. How would you summarize God's instructions in Cornelius' vision?

Read Acts 10:9-16. How would you summarize God's instructions in Peter's vision?

How does Peter initially react? Why do you think he reacts this way?

The food laws that the Israelites obeyed were vast and strict. You can see some of them in Leviticus 11. The purpose of the laws was to keep Israel holy – to set them apart – so that they would be different from the other nations and peoples living around them.

God wanted Israel to be different from the rest of the world because God was revealing himself through Israel, and God is different than the world. Peter's reaction is so strong because Peter wants to be holy. He has spent his entire life believing and trying to avoid everything that God is now telling him to do.

Read Acts 10:15 again. How does God respond to Peter's objection?

What does God's response tell us about who the kingdom of God is for?

Are there other countries in our world that Christians seem to look down on or consider our enemies? Who are they?

Why do you think we separate from them?

One statistic that we are having a hard time figuring out is related to how many Christians there are in the Middle East. Large numbers of people have denounced Islam and accepted Jesus Christ as their Lord and Savior, but refuse to be called Christians because they don't want to be associated with the immorality of the United States of America.[3] In other words, to them, we are Rome.

How does that make you feel?

In what ways have you seen our nationalism hurt our Christian witness today?

Read Acts 10:39-48. As Peter meets Cornelius, and he understands what God is doing, he makes this incredible claim that "everyone" who believes in Jesus receives forgiveness of sins through His name. Who is excluded here?

---

[3] Tennent, Timothy (2007). Theology in the Context of World Christianity. Zondervan, Grand Rapids, MI.

Both Peter and Cornelius had to be humbled by God before they could embrace God's kingdom. How was Peter humbled?

How was Cornelius humbled?

How or where might we need to be humbled so that we can embrace the truth and mission of God's kingdom?

Think about your own prejudices. Who do you exclude from the kingdom of God simply because they are from a different country, a different ethnicity, or a different lifestyle than yours?

What message might God have for you about those people?

This week, spend time in prayer each day, asking God to reveal your prejudices and to give you the courage and faith to believe and grow like Peter.

the kingdom for all peoples

Acts 14:8-18

—

As I have grown older, there is a habit that I've tried to break, but sneaks back into my life every once in a while. I used to pray for my sports team to win.

I have realized, first, that in the grand scheme of things, who wins a basketball game doesn't really matter. But I've also realized that for every prayer I lift up in support of my team, there are probably just as many being lifted up in support of the other. Does God love Indiana more than Purdue? Duke more than North Carolina? I guess it depends on who you ask and who won the last game.

It is this kind of question, though, that the early apostles faced as the Good News of Jesus spread out of the Jewish faith and into the rest of the world.

If God really does love the whole world, why the exclusive relationship with Israel? Why was God only rooting for one team?

In our text today, Paul gets to answer this question in an exciting and wild turn of events.

Read Acts 14:8-10. Try to put yourself in the crowd that day… When you saw this miracle, how would you react? What would you think?

Read Acts 14:11-13. How do the people living in Lystra react?

Read Acts 14:14-18. How do Barnabas and Paul respond to the crowd's worship?

Look at verse 15. What do they tell us about God?

Look at verses 16-17. What do they say here about God's love for the whole world?

Paul says that God's testimony to the world outside of Israel was his kindness. What does this teach us about what life in the Kingdom of God looks like?

Think about your own life. In what ways did God show you his kindness before you knew him?

What might this teach us about how we should treat non-believers today?

Are there people in this world that we believe don't deserve kindness? Who are they? Why do we think that way?

How might sharing the Gospel with non-believers go better if we paired our verbal witness with acts of loving kindness?

What is one thing that you will do this week to show the kindness of God to a non-believer that you know in your life?

the kingdom for every person

Romans 1:8-17

—

"Nobody owes nobody nothin'. You owe yourself. Friends don't owe! They do because they wanna do."

Rocky Balboa spoke those words in Rocky III. Today, they hang on posters, are printed on t-shirts, and speak to a sentiment that many of us feel in our lives. I don't owe anyone anything. I work hard for my money. I earned what I have. Yeah, I'll help a friend if I want to, maybe, but I'm indebted to no one.

This way of thinking is a result of the American dream. Ironically, it stands in contrast to the dream of America's founders.

It was George Washington who wrote, in a letter to Alexander Hamilton, that, "It may be laid down as a primary position, and the basis of our system, that every citizen who enjoys the protection of a free government, owes not only a portion of his property, but even of his personal services to the defense of it."

In other words, Washington felt that citizens of the U.S.A. have an obligation to pay taxes and serve our country in any way necessary because of the protections and life that our country provides us.

In our text today, we see Paul applying a similar way of thinking to his role as a follower of Jesus Christ.

Read Romans 1:8-13. Why is Paul thankful for the Christians in Rome?

Why does he long to visit them so badly?

How would you describe Paul's feelings for the Christians in Rome?

What does this teach us about how we should feel about each other as fellow Christians?

Read Romans 1:14-15. What are some of the obligations that you have in life? How would you define an obligation?

The word Paul uses for obligation literally means, "indebted." Who is Paul obligated or indebted to?

What is the obligation that he must fulfill? How does he pay the debt that he carries?

Do you get the sense that Paul sees sharing the Gospel with others as an option for Christians or as a requirement? Why do you think so?

In Paul's world, most people had a worldview that split the world into two categories. You were either a Greek, or you weren't. You were either an uncivilized barbarian, or you were cultured and wise. When Paul speaks of being obligated to both Greeks and non-Greeks, both to the wise and the foolish, he is leaving no one out. His obligation was to everyone – not just the Jews, not just to Christians, not just to the Romans… but to every person, regardless of who they are or where they are from.

This is powerful. Some of us feel obligated to evangelize and disciple our children, our families, and maybe our friends… but a stranger? A foreigner? An enemy?

In your life, do you approach sharing the Gospel with others like Rocky – like you don't owe it to anyone – or like Paul – like you are indebted to everyone? Why do you think so?

Do you feel indebted to some people, but not others? Why does this happen?

What does Paul's sense of obligation to every person teach us about what life in the kingdom of God is like?

Read 1 Timothy 1:15. How do you think Paul's understanding of himself as the worst of sinners increased his sense of obligation and indebtedness to share the Gospel with others?

This week, write 1 Timothy 1:15 down somewhere you will see it every day. Take a picture of it and set it as your home screen on your phone. Do something to remind you to read and pray this scripture passage each day.

As you pray, ask God to increase your love for him and your appreciation of what he has done for you.

Finally, pray that he would increase your love for every person – not just people like you, not just people close to you, but people everywhere.

the kingdom for sinners

Romans 5:1-11

—

Read Romans 5:1-11. Look at the passage as a whole. As Paul describes the progression that we go through as followers of Christ, how would you describe the starting line? Who are we before we know Jesus?

How would you describe the finish line? What does peace with God mean?

How does Paul think we should respond to such incredible news?

What does it mean to boast?

Read Romans 5:6-8. Who/what should be the object and topic of our boasting?

When you talk to others about God, how often do you mention your sinfulness? Why is this an important part of our story?

Why do we tend to leave it out?

Read verses 3-5 again. What does Paul say is the final result of suffering?

How might sharing your personal stories of how Christ gave you perseverance, character, and hope through a time of suffering bring hope to another person?

How might sharing your salvation story and boasting about how Christ rescued you from sin and death bring hope to a non-believer?

Were you a sinner or were you righteous when Christ died for you?

What does this teach us about what life in the Kingdom of God looks like?

If we have received reconciliation with God, if we have been justified through faith, if we have peace with God and stand in his grace, we are certainly expected to pursue righteousness and repent of all sin.

However, it is also always important to remember that there is no one who enters the Kingdom of God who did not need Jesus to die for them so that they could enter.

How would remembering this help us boast in Christ instead of ourselves?

How would remembering this help us treat each other better?

How would remembering this help us to treat non-believers better?

This week, pay attention to what you boast in. What dominates your conversations? What dominates your social media posts?

What is one thing that you can do this week to boast in Christ by sharing your own personal story?

36618229R00042

Made in the USA
Middletown, DE
15 February 2019